TOPICS IN MEDIEVAL HISTORY
Edited by DAVID J. HALL

People and Places/GILLIAN DAY

WITH DRAWINGS BY ROY SCHOFIELD

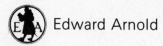 Edward Arnold

© Gillian Day 1974
First published 1974
by Edward Arnold (Publishers) Ltd.,
25 Hill Street, London W1X 8LL

ISBN: 0 7131 1831 8

Set in 10 on 12 pt. Univers light by Keyspools Limited, Golborne, Lancs
and printed in Great Britain by Butler & Tanner Ltd., Frome

Contents

Acknowledgments

The Publisher's thanks are due to the following for permission to use photographs reproduced in this book:

Mansell Collection (pp. 7, 9, 11, 12, 20, 25, 29 *bottom*, 30, 32, 36, 38, 40 *bottom*);

British Museum (pp. 8 *right*, 22, 24, 26, 29 *top*, 31, 42 *right*, 43);

Radio Times Hulton Picture Library (pp. 13, 15 *left and right*, 16 *left*, 19, 21, 43 *left*);

Herbert Felton (p. 16 *right*);

National Portrait Gallery (p. 23 *top*);

Keystone Press Agency (pp. 23 *bottom*, 27);

Brian Shuel (p. 33 *top and bottom*);

Bibliothèque Royale, Brussels (p. 39);

The Times (pp. 40 *top*, 41).

Thanks are also due to the author and publisher of *Brasses* and *Brass Rubbing* by Clare Gittings (Blandford Press) for permission to reproduce photographs on pp. 8 (*left*), 44 (*right*) and 45 (*left*), and to the author and publisher of *Brass Rubbing* by Malcolm Norris (Studio Vista) for permission to reproduce photographs on pp. 45 (*right*) and 47.

To the Reader

This book describes People and Places from the Norman Conquest to
A.D. 1500 — the Middle Ages or medieval times as it is often called.

The information is given in the written part of each chapter and in the
photographs, drawings and descriptions of the pictures. At the end of each
section there are questions for you to answer in your note books. You will
also find it helpful to copy some of the drawings into your books.

You should compare present day people and places with those described
in the book. List all the differences and try to find out why they have
changed. Your teacher will help you to do this.

1 Clothes and Faces

In medieval times people looked old at a much earlier age than they do now. This was partly because there was no real cure for skin diseases and partly because there were no medicines to ease the pain of illness. Suffering showed in people's faces. Black, broken teeth, sores, spots or smallpox scars had marked the faces of rich and poor by their early teens. Broken legs were not mended and straightened properly so it was usual to see many poor people with twisted legs as crippled as those in the drawing.

The poet Chaucer described one of his pilgrims who had "a flaming red face, black scabby eyebrows so that children were scared by his face". It was hard to tell by looking at a man's face how wealthy he was but his clothes showed exactly his importance. Poor peasants were only allowed to wear clothes made from "blanket and russet wool at five pence a metre". Nobles, on the other hand, could choose from many materials including bright coloured velvet, silks and satin. There were no shops which sold ready made clothes in medieval times. So most people made their tunics and dresses at home from raw wool spun by the women into rough grey cloth. If, however, the buyer was rich enough, he went to a tailor. The tailor and his apprentices cut and sewed clothes from smooth cloth, taking care to obey certain rules. These rules described the types of fur used to line and trim the robes to keep people warm in their cold and draughty houses. The king wore ermine fur, his nobles squirrel and sable, and ordinary folk rabbit, cat or sheepskin. These rules also said that only the king and the nobles could wear long robes and cloaks. Merchants were allowed to wear calf-length robes and working men wore short, knee-length tunics. A poor person could also wear leggings, and a short cape called a capuchon, which had a hood to keep his head and ears warm. Rich and poor alike looked after their clothes for they were expensive and took a long time to make. They lasted for many years because one story tells us about an innkeeper's wife who wore the same shapeless dress for forty years! Shoes wore out more quickly. Rich people wore soft leather boots, poor folk had boots made of thick felt. In winter and wet weather most people changed into wooden clogs before stepping through the mud.

Things to do

1 *Complete these sentences using the words in the box.*
People looked .... at an earlier age than they do now.
There were no .... which sold ready made clothes.
The king wore .... fur and ....clothes.
Poor people wore .... fur and .... tunics.

2 Working men wore short tunics

3 Capuchon and clogs

4 A tailor making clothes

```
shops, long, rabbit, old,
ermine, short
```

2 *Why was it easy to tell how rich a man was by looking at his clothes?*

3 *Why did people often look old at an early age?*

2 Fashionable Clothes for Rich People

Only rich people could buy the fine cloth trimmed with jewels used by medieval tailors. Poor people lived in the same shabby clothes which their parents had worn. The wealthy liked wearing their colourful clothes but they also hoped that these clothes would increase in value as time went on. They always left careful instructions in their wills saying which relatives should have their robes, cloaks and tunics. In the early years of the Middle Ages those clothes were still simple and allowed people to move quickly and easily. Women wore long, tight-sleeved dresses and graceful head-dresses whilst men had robes with wide sleeves that touched the ground.

Gradually styles grew more extravagant, and more decorated, and the only aim of the new designs was to show the wealth and importance of the wearer. Indeed only rich people with a lot of spare time could wear these clothes because they took so long to put on. A young man wore a short pleated tunic, edged with fur, with a padded chest and tight belt. His shoes of soft leather had long pointed toes up to thirty centimetres long. He filled the toes with moss to make them curve upwards so that the young man looked as though he was standing on skiis! It was almost impossible to climb upstairs in the shoes unless he walked backwards! A writer called Hoccleve described one man, "walking about in a scarlet robe eleven metres wide with sleeves trailing on the ground and covered with costly furs". He did not like this waste of money and said crossly that tailors would soon have to cut and fold the material in the fields because their workshops were too small for such large patterns!

Women now wore either a tall pointed head-dress with a veil or a pair of wire "wings" holding a long muslin veil, called a "butterfly head-dress". They had to wear corsets of wood to squeeze themselves into narrow waisted dresses. It was fashionable to have a broad forehead so women combed their hair back from

2 Cosmetics

1 Lady Elizabeth Cobham. A simple style of dress

their faces and sometimes shaved off their eyebrows. You can see in the picture a lady combing her hair with the help of the maid who holds a mirror. She kept red and white face powder in the box on the floor, for just as they do today, women in the Middle Ages spent a lot of time changing the colour of their faces.

Things to do

1 *Complete these sentences using the words in the box.*

In early medieval times rich people wore .... styles of clothes.
Later styles were more ....
The tall head-dress in the picture is called a .... head-dress.
Women used .... to colour their faces.

extravagant, butterfly, powder, simple

2 *Why do you think the writer Hoccleve complained about the man in the scarlet robe?*
3 *Why could only rich people wear the fashionable clothes of the later Middle Ages?*

3   Butterfly head-dresses

4   Rich men and women wearing fashionable clothes at the end of the Middle Ages

9

3 The Housewife

1 A kitchen

In medieval days a girl usually married as soon as the parents could find her a husband, because the only other way of life for her was to become a nun or stay a spinster. The girl married her husband without complaining, even if she did not like him much, for everyone felt sorry for unmarried girls. A wife's duty was to look after her husband, and his house, and buy and cook all the food. We would call her a "housewife" now, but in the Middle Ages her job was harder than it is today. Housework and cooking meals was difficult and she had no machines to help her in the house. Farmers had not discovered a way of feeding their farm animals in winter and so they killed most of them at the end of the summer. This meant that every summer the housewife had to worry about what her family would eat in the winter time. She added salt to the meat and stored it, with dried salted fish, grain and barrels of beer. When the time came to eat this meat and fish, she added spices to hide its horrid salty taste.

Pepper, ginger, cloves and cinnamon spices were expensive because they came from abroad, and dockers unloading the spice ships had to wear suits without pockets so that they couldn't hide any spices they stole. Cooking was all done on a bright fire in the kitchen. The housewife roasted fresh meat in summer on a spit, as you can see in the picture, and boiled salted meat in a cooking pot hanging over the fire. She used a flesh hook, a long fork with a wooden handle, to pull the cooked meat out of the pot. The housewife baked pies, cakes and bread in an oven to one side of the fire. It was just a hole in the wall, closed with an iron door, but it made good bread. The family ate most of the food at 11 o'clock in the morning. This was the main meal of the day although there was a little more food for supper at 4 o'clock in the afternoon. People do not seem to have eaten much breakfast, and were content with a drink of beer and some bread. So the perfect wife worked hard to look after her house. Many wives, however, spent their time in other ways. They dressed in fashionable clothes and powdered their faces with white flour. The priests were annoyed with wives who wore yellow dresses, calling them "yellow frogs", and told other wives not to wear make-up ("the devil's soap") nor to spend so long in front of their mirrors ("the devil's hiding place"). Many wives who knew that their husbands did not like them to go out at all, kept a pet animal for company while they had to stay at home. They liked dogs best, as you see in the picture, but they also kept nightingales, parrots, squirrels and even monkeys. Housewives used cats to catch mice but cats were not treated as pets.

Things to do

1 Complete these sentences using the words in the box.

A girl married a husband chosen by her ....
The housewife used .... and .... spices to flavour her cooking.
The main meal of the day was eaten at .... o'clock in the morning.
Housewives kept pet animals such as ...., but never ....

> pepper, dogs, eleven, family, cats, ginger

2 In what ways was the work of a medieval housewife different from the work of a modern wife?

2 Housewife and dog

4 Meat cooking in a pot

3 Meat cooking on a spit

4 A Young Housewife

1 Flies

2 Fleas

3 Marriage

We know exactly what life in the Middle Ages was like for one young housewife, because her husband wrote a book for her called "An Introduction to the Whole Art of Being a Wife, a Housewife and a Perfect Lady". When she married, the girl was fifteen and her husband was over sixty. So she asked him to write some notes on how to run the house, and those notes became the book. In each chapter he told his wife that she must always be loving and patient with him. She must be ready to forgive him, no matter how badly he behaved. He was fond of telling his poor wife about the faithful dog which was obedient even for its cruel master! He warned her that three things would make him leave home. They were, a dripping roof, a smoking chimney and a cross, nagging wife. If the young wife followed all these instructions and was a perfect wife then, as a special reward, her husband promised never to shout at her in front of strangers. He would of course still shout at her when they were alone together! The book described all the work that had to be done each day. First, at six o'clock the young wife had to tidy her hair, smooth down the collar of her dress and walk to Church "with eyelids low and not fluttering, looking straight in front about four rods (eight paces) ahead, without speaking to anyone on the road". After Church she worked in the house, making certain her servants swept and dusted and killed all the flies in the rooms. She made a special effort to get rid of fleas. She found those in the bedclothes by placing a white sheet on top of the bed so that the black fleas were easy to see and kill when they jumped onto the sheet. Those fleas living in clothes were more difficult to find. She and her maids took all the dresses and furs into the garden, shook them and spread them out in the sun. Then they put the clothes away rolled up tightly in bags, hoping that any fleas still around would die without light and air. The young wife spent a lot of her time cooking for the main meal of the day at eleven o'clock in the morning. The husband's recipes did not give his wife exact cooking times, for she had no clocks of the sort we use today. Instead, she had to cook a sauce "for as long as it takes to say a Paternoster" (a prayer). After the meal, the afternoon was the young wife's time to enjoy her-

4 A walled garden

5 A special meal

self. She sometimes gossiped and entertained friends in her small walled garden, or went out hawking with them. If nobody came to see her, she picked violets and roses which grew in the garden or sewed colourful pictures to hang on the walls of her house. Her day ended when it grew dark, and she and her husband made certain that the servants were asleep, then they locked all the doors before they too went to bed.

Things to do

1   *Complete these sentences using the words in the box.*
We know about life in the Middle Ages for one young housewife because her husband wrote a .... for her.
The young wife went to ....
every morning.

She had to remove .... from clothing and bedding.
She enjoyed herself gossiping with friends or out ....

fleas, hawking, Church, book

2   *What were the three things which would make the young wife's husband leave home?*

5 Hawking and Gambling

1 Hawking

Both rich and poor people killed small animals like rabbits for food. There were also many duck, partridge, heron and pigeon in the countryside, but it was not easy to catch them. If they were too far away, or flew too quickly for an arrow to reach them, then only a bird which could fly faster could catch them. People chose falcons to do this chasing. Falcons have short hooked beaks and strong claws so they can catch and kill slower birds. Wild falcons only kill when they are hungry. So the falconer had to find them when they were very young, tame them, and then teach them to catch birds and small animals that he wanted to eat. The falconer tied a new young bird to his wrist and it sat on his gloved hand nearly all day. Some people even kept their falcons in their bedrooms at night, perched on a special bar next to the rail where they hung their own clothes! After getting used to his master in this way, the falcon was taken outside. It had a decorated hood over its head to stop it seeing and attacking other birds. As soon as the falconer saw a pigeon he wanted for food, he pointed the falcon at it and took off its hood. Then the falcon flew off, caught the pigeon, pulled it down out of the sky and killed it. Dogs ran to collect the body and the falcon flew back to its master. You can imagine that very great care was taken of these valuable birds. People did not allow servants who had fleas to look after their falcons in case the birds caught the fleas! When the birds were really ill, their owners made a pilgrimage to a shrine to pray for their recovery. The Abbot of Westminster even left a wax model of his sick falcon at the shrine when he called there to ask for it to be cured. The Abbot, because he was a priest, was allowed to own a sparrow hawk, but servants could only keep kestrels. More important people could keep better types of falcon. A noble owned a peregrine falcon, which killed birds much larger than itself, and the King kept the best of all, a Gyr falcon. This rule of ownership was most important when a stray falcon was found. The finder gave this bird to the Sheriff. If no one claimed it within four months, he could keep it, but only if it was the right type of bird. If a servant found a rich man's peregrine falcon, the Sheriff paid him a money reward instead, and kept the peregrine himself. Sometimes a valuable falcon was stolen. The Bishop of Lincoln excommunicated a whole village because he thought the villagers had hidden Sir Gerald Salvayh's best peregrine falcon. During the winter evenings when it was too dark for hawking, falconers played games of dice, cards and chess. It may seem surprising, but the quiet game of chess often ended in a riot. People betted on who would win, and the loser and his friends who had lost money on the chess match then started a fight.

14

2 A Peregrine Falcon

A falconer's hand and glove

4 Gambling

3 Chess

Kings and nobles were allowed to own .... and .... falcons.

falconer, peregrine, falcons, valuable, Gyr

Things to do

1 *Complete these sentences using the words in the box.*
People used .... to catch wild birds and small animals.
A .... trained the young birds.
A well-trained falcon was very ....

2 *How do sportsmen now catch wild birds and rabbits?*

3 *Describe in your own words how a falcon was trained and cared for by the falconer.*

15

6 The Household of Richard Swinfield

1 A moated manor house, Stokesay Castle

3 Inside the Great Hall at Stokesay Castle

Richard Swinfield was Bishop of Hereford and a very rich man. He owned houses in Hereford, Worcester and London, and land in three counties, Herefordshire, Gloucestershire and Shropshire. His farms supplied enough meat and eggs for his household with some left over to feed the poor people who waited outside his house at meal times. On Easter Day, 1290, the Bishop's household used 1,400 eggs. We know the exact number because there is a record of his housekeeping costs from Autumn 1289 to Autumn 1290, written down on an eight metre roll of parchment (dried animal skin). We know how much he paid each servant and that he kept a special servant to look after his horses and collect wood for the fires. Another important servant, called Adam Harpin, trained the falcons. Adam kept watch in June on the birds' nests, caught the young ones then tamed and trained them for the Bishop. Later, in Autumn, he used them, and nets, to catch partridge for the banquets in Hereford. For his good work and long service of fifteen years, he was given a cottage at Ross-on-Wye owned by the Bishop for a rent of just twenty-two pence a year.

The parchment shows that musicians and jugglers entertained at the Hereford house, but the Bishop did not spend much time there to enjoy their jokes. He had to travel to see and talk to his priests personally, for there were no telephones to make his work easier. The first journey lasted from October until Christmas, for the Bishop was an old man and only liked to travel twelve miles each day. At each manor house where the household stopped on the journey, servants took all the luggage from the packhorses and bullock carts so that Richard Swinfield had a comfortable stay.

At some of these houses he went hawking, but at other times he bought clothes and household goods. We know that he sent two servants, Ralph and John, to buy barrels of good wine for him in Bristol. You can see one of them tasting the wine. The Bishop spent Christmas at a stone manor house which was surrounded by a moat and looked like Stokesay Castle shown on the opposite page. He was soon on the road again after Christmas, and travelled this time with a convoy of 51 horses and many carts to his house in Old Fish Street, London. While he was in London he met the King and Queen in their new Palace at Westminster. On the way back to Herefordshire the Bishop visited Ross-on-Wye and looked at his prison there. This was a prison without a normal door, the only way in and out was through a trap-door in the high ceiling. Clerks imprisoned there had little chance of escape! The Bishop called on the Abbot of Wigmore, a lazy priest who often forgot to preach in Church, and as the parchment says "scolded him" (told him off). These visits to his priests took Richard Swinfield many weeks so it was May before he reached Hereford again and began his

3   Bullocks and carts

preparations for another expedition in the Autumn.

4   Tasting the wine

Things to do

1   Complete these sentences using the words in the box.
Richard Swinfield was Bishop of
....
We have a record of his .... costs written on a roll of parchment.
.... trained the Bishop's falcons.
After Christmas the Bishop travelled to ....

Adam Harpin, London, Hereford, household

2   Why was it difficult for clerks to escape from the Bishop's prison at Ross-on-Wye?

17

7 Christmas

1 Christmas dinner

2 Boar's head

Christmas in the Middle Ages was a time for presents, eating good food and above all enjoying oneself, but the food, the games and the idea of Father Christmas were all different from a modern Christmas. Children did not look forward to seeing a "Father Christmas" but waited for a kindly old man very like him with a bushy white beard and red cloak called St Nicholas. They thought this saint was a good priest who loved them and left small gifts at Christmas time. The naughty ones were frightened of his servant who had orders to smack them so that they would be good in the following year.

On Christmas Day itself guests came to the party wearing masks. They soon joined in the jokes and games organised by one of the servants. He was chosen as "King of Christmas" and called "the Lord of Misrule". His job was to lead the fun and everybody, including his master, had to obey him. The wilder the games and the more cheeky his jokes, the more they cheered him on. If the Lord of Misrule was wise, he was careful not to be too cheeky or else, when Christmas was over, his master might have his revenge and punish him.

The meal began at mid-day and lasted for eight or nine hours. In a rich man's house trumpet blasts from the musicians welcomed the servants as they carried in each new plate of food. The musicians played throughout the meal, but their loudest trumpeting came when the chief cook proudly carried in the boar's head, (wild pig's head). The guests ate mince-pies, minced meat mixed with spice and covered in a pastry crust. The pie, baked in a dish shaped like a manger, had a small figure of Jesus on top. Lastly they ate plum porridge, real porridge with raisins, spices and fruit juices mixed into it and, perhaps more important, silver pennies and gifts hidden inside. People believed that guests who found the silver coins could buy good luck with them and the girl who found the silver ring would soon find a husband as well. After the meal, guests joined in more games. They played "hoodman blind" in which one person turned his hood over his face and had to catch someone to take his place. Those who found this too noisy took part in special Christmas songs and dances called "caroles". The guests sang as they danced slowly in a circle, as you see in the picture.

Things to do

1   *Complete these sentences using the words in the box.*
    Saint .... left presents for children at Christmas.
    The ....
    was a servant chosen as "King of Christmas".
    A .... was a special Christmas dance and song.

    > Lord of Misrule, Nicholas, carole

2   *What seems to be the same and what seems different about Christmas today and the Christmas described here?*

3   A carole

4   St Nicholas

5   Hoodman Blind

19

8 Children

1   Babies in swaddling clothes

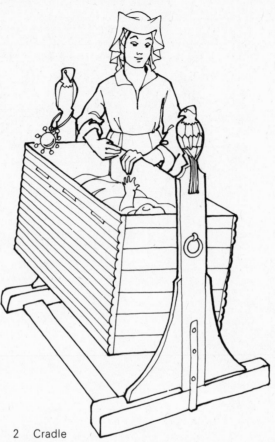

2   Cradle

In medieval times mothers wrapped their babies in bandages, believing it would make their legs grow straight. So a child spent the first months of his life in a neat parcel, unable to move anything but his head. The mother carried her young baby easily, for these bandages called swaddling clothes supported the baby's weak legs and back. The baby slept in a wooden cradle on which the mother put a silver rattle to keep evil spirits away. As soon as children could walk they wore the same kind of clothes as grown-ups.

Girls wore long dresses, boys had short pleated tunics with padded chests, big sleeves and tight belts. As well as dressing like adults, children had to behave like them too. If they did not, their parents hit them, "with a smart rod 'till they cry for mercy". All children had to obey their parents, and many parents were as strict as Agnes Paston who beat her daughter once or twice every week! However, the children did enjoy themselves sometimes! You can see in the picture the games they played. A boy is sitting on a swing and he watches someone playing skittles. Another boy plays with a whip and top while his friend walks on stilts. The time children really liked was the Spring when the days grew longer, and parents took them to the May Festivals. On 1 May, the start of summer, young children collected tree branches and decorated them with bunches of flowers. They put the bunches round the doors and windows of all the houses except those of unpopular neighbours, who found their windows covered with nettles! The children then danced with the Morris Dancers who wore bells on their legs and sometimes dressed up as horses, unicorns, clowns or dragons.

You can still see Morris Dancers at Thaxted in Essex and the photo shows you the Unicorn of the Westminster Morris men. After the dances they chose a pretty girl as the May Queen and a boy as Lord of the May. Both dressed in white and wore crowns. One dance at every spring festival took place round a tall, painted pole decorated with flowers called a maypole. Each parish had its own pole which was carried through the town before the dancing started. The pole or shaft that was used in front of St Andrew's Church in London was so tall that the Church was called St Andrew Undershaft. Although children played and enjoyed themselves as children do today, in one way they were very different. Rich children were quite often married before they were four. Their families arranged these marriages to settle debts or to make certain that two families stayed friendly. Grace de Saleby had married three husbands by the time she was eleven. Often the children did not know what the words of the marriage ceremony meant. The priest carried one three year old bridegroom, John Rigmarden, into Church. John forgot his words but remembered them quickly when the priest promised that he could go back and play with his friends as soon as the service ended!

Things to do

1 *Complete these sentences using the words in the box.*
   Mothers wrapped their babies in bandages called ...., ...
   Boys and girls wore the .... kind of clothes as grown-ups.

3   Children playing games

Dancers called ....
dressed up as horses, unicorns and clowns.
Rich children married when they were very ....

> same, Morris Dancers, young,
> swaddling clothes

2 *How many different sorts of games can you see in the picture at the top of this page? Are any of them still played today?*

4   Unicorn of Westminster Morris Men

9 Lady Anne Mowbray

1 A bedroom

2 The Tower of London

Lady Anne Mowbray lived at the end of the Middle Ages. Her family were rich and so she was able to have many more things than other girls of her age, but she liked the same sort of things as all children living then. She was born in a bedroom like the one you can see in the picture, and lived at Framlingham Castle in Suffolk. We know she went to Church every day, and with her family made the pilgrimage to the shrine of St Thomas à Becket at Canterbury.

When they went on a journey, such as a pilgrimage, the family took many carts with them to carry cooking pots, clothes, furniture and even the tapestry pictures from the castle walls. As soon as she could walk, Lady Anne was given her own special servants and teachers to look after her. She had waiting maids to fetch and carry for her and sewing maids to make her clothes. She had a priest and teacher to help her with her books and a small friend of her own age to play with her. Together the girls watched jugglers, acrobats, and the dancing bears who came to the castle.

Most of all they looked forward to Christmas when they played all sorts of noisy games. When she was three her father, the Duke of Norfolk, died and left Anne a lot of money and land. Now she was the richest girl in England. So King Edward IV, who wanted a bride for his son Richard, arranged with Anne's mother for the children to marry. The parents talked about the details for a long time but at last both families were happy. Richard, Duke of York, and Anne married in St Stephen's Chapel at Westminster Palace when she was five and he was just four.

Anne, now Countess of Surrey and Duchess of York, gave out the prizes at the tournament held in her honour that afternoon. Three years later, Anne died, and the King gave his daughter-in-law an expensive funeral. Three barges followed the boat carrying her body up the River from Greenwich to London. No one knew exactly where she was buried until 1964 when builders found her small lead coffin on their building site in Stepney. She has now been re-buried in Westminster Abbey. After Anne's death, her family were mixed up in many quarrels. All but two of the important guests at her wedding were murdered or died in strange circumstances, (Uncle George drowned in a barrel of wine!). Anne's husband and his brother were put in the Tower of London by their Uncle Richard of Gloucester. Some say he arranged the murder of the two little Princes in the Tower because he wanted them out of the way so that he could be King instead.

Things to do

1   Complete these sentences using the words in the box.
Lady Anne lived at .... Castle in Suffolk.
She married .... Duke of York when she was .... and he was .... years old.
In 1964, her body was found on a building site at .... in London.

> five, Richard, four, Stepney, Framlingham

2   What happened later to Lady Anne's husband, and to most of their wedding guests?

3   Richard of Gloucester

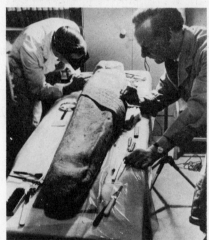

4   Lady Anne's coffin

5   Lady Anne Mowbray's shoes

10 Schools

All children in the Middle Ages were shown how to do things but very few read books to teach themselves. Boys from wealthy families learnt to read and write from the family priest at home. Afterwards they were sent to another rich household, sometimes as pages, to learn about fighting, hawking, hunting and good manners. Their sisters stayed with the parents and learnt from their mothers how to cook and sew. Few girls could read as this was thought dangerous and unnecessary—"it is better if women can nought of it!" Foreigners thought the English were cruel to send their sons away from home and the Ambassador from Venice, Andrea Trevisan, said how strict fathers and mothers were in England. You can understand how careful children had to be when you read the letters written by the young Paston boys which started, "Right reverend and worshipful father"! In the towns, merchants sent their sons to schools where they got the same harsh treatment as boys in rich households. The Grammar schools, so called because Latin Grammar was the main subject, consisted of a single room with one master teaching twenty-five or thirty boys of all ages.

Boys went to school all day from Monday to Saturday, and for half of Sunday as well. Lessons started at 6 o'clock and carried on until 9 o'clock. Then followed a short break for prayers,

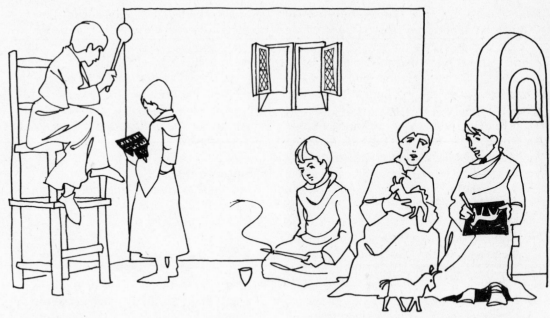

1   Boys pretending to be at school

fifteen minutes for breakfast, and lessons again until 11 o'clock. After dinner lessons in winter lasted from 1 o'clock until 5, but in summer there was longer free time until 3 o'clock. Then there was a quick drink of beer and lessons finally finished at 7. Boys spent all this time learning Latin poetry, translating Latin stories and speaking in Latin, for they did not use English at all in school.

The schoolmaster had the only books so his pupils had to listen to him and learn things by heart. They copied books, writing with a feather pen onto paper made from animal skins. You can see a picture of the master showing boys how to write.

Some pupils, like John Lydgate in King's Lynn, did not like school at all. He wrote that he was "loth (unwilling) to lerne", and "hadde in custom to come to scole late". He talked in school, told lies and pretended to be ill to miss his classes.

Schoolmasters punished boys like John, hitting them with a cane or palmer (a rod with a flat wooden disc at the end used for smacking boys' hands). In the picture of boys pretending to be at school, the "master" in the chair is ready with the palmer! The teacher used the cane and palmer to punish every small mistake and,

2 A writing lesson

3 A game of hockey

4 A game of bat and ball

before taking his Degree, had to show he could use the cane properly. Although some pupils did not like the lessons they all enjoyed the games they played. The pictures show children playing hockey and bat and ball. Some other sports, such as teams on horseback fighting each other and bear baiting are not now allowed in school!

Things to do

1 *Complete these sentences using the words in the box.*
   Merchants sent their sons to .... schools.
   Pupils copied books, writing with a .... pen onto paper made from ....
   Teachers used the cane and .... to punish every small mistake.
   It was thought dangerous to teach .... to read!

girls, feather, palmer, Grammar, animal skins

2 *Point out some differences between schools in the Middle Ages and schools now. Has anything remained the same?*

11 Students

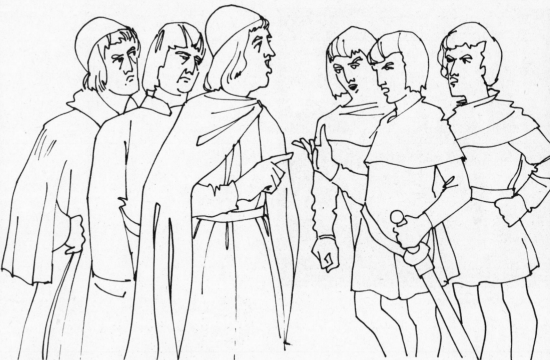

1   Students working

2   Students quarrel with the townsmen

Medieval students were often only twelve to fourteen years old, much younger than students are today. They had to work hard. Agnes Paston wrote to her son's teacher at Cambridge asking him "to be-lash him till he will amend" (do better) if her son Clement did not learn his work. One of the young men at Oxford, Friar Roger Bacon, was a clever scientist. He thought about how things happened and how things worked, and through his studying said that one day engines would drive ships and carts. But he could not make these engines, or the flying machines he said might carry men through the sky. We think he invented gunpowder in Europe, although the Chinese knew about it many years beforehand. For all his modern thinking, Roger still believed that the Earth was the centre of the Universe, that it was flat, and that the City of Jerusalem stood at its centre! The picture opposite shows Roger's study on Folly Bridge in Oxford. It stayed on the Bridge until engineers in the eighteenth century pulled it down to widen the road. Sometimes, however, the townspeople fell out with the students and fought them in the streets.

In Oxford and Cambridge the students wandered about after dark in bands of "nightwalkers", annoying people. In 1209 the townsmen of Oxford hanged two students who had murdered a woman. The picture shows the students and townsfolk facing each other and it is not surprising that the rows sometimes ended in death, as both sides used swords, daggers or bows and arrows in the fighting. However there was a more pleasant side to the life of youngsters in medieval days. Each year at St Paul's School in London the boys chose a pupil to be the "Boy Bishop" and he chose some of his own friends to be the Bishop's priests. They dressed in small copies of the clothes worn by the real priests and the Boy Bishop wore a gold ring and pointed hat called a mitre. The boys took over the Cathedral on 6 December, the Feast of Holy Innocents, and the Boy Bishop preached the sermon. Afterwards he rode through the streets of London giving people his blessing and collecting money for his Church and School. If he was unlucky enough to die while playing this part, he had the same expensive funeral that would be given to the real Bishop. The ceremony of the Boy Bishop still takes place as you can see from the picture of a thirteen-year-old "Bishop" from London.

Things to do

1 *Complete these sentences using the words in the box.*
The Boy Bishop preached the sermon on the Feast of ....
Townsfolk and .... sometimes fought in the streets.
.... was a clever scientist.
He thought that one day ....
would drive ships and carts.

Roger Bacon, students, Holy Innocents, engines

2 *Roger Bacon had some modern ideas for transport. How many of his ideas have we used today?*

3 The Boy Bishop

4 Roger Bacon's study on Folly Bridge

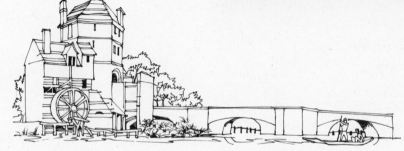

27

12 The Black Death

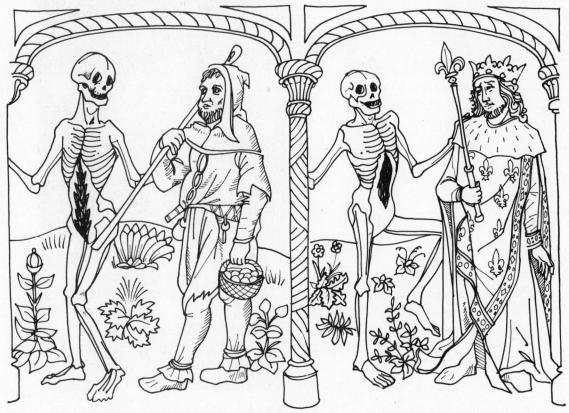

1   The Dance of Death

in again. Nearby at Steeple Barton, thirty-six of the villagers died, the water mill lay in ruins and more than six hundred acres of farm land was left untended. All fifty-two tenants who lived at Tilgarsley had died, for in 1359 a tax collector reported that no one had lived there for the past nine years. No one was safe, for if you look at the picture at the top of this page you will see that it makes it very clear the Black Death killed rich men as well as poor men.

No one felt safe. Some prayed, but many decided to enjoy what might be their last few hours, "Eat, drink and be merry, for tomorrow we die" was their motto.

2   Plague victim

The Black Death or Bubonic Plague reached Dorset on the South coast of England in 1348, probably brought by sailors. People who caught the plague sneezed, became feverish and had painful red boils and large black spots on their bodies, usually dying within a few days.

The disease spread quickly through England and very few towns escaped. One person in every three died, including half the population of London. In some villages, like Tusmore near Oxford, everyone died and the village was never lived

The germs which caused the Black Death were spread by rat fleas. Medieval doctors did not know this and tried some of the following cures. They said that cooked onions mixed with butter should be put on the boils, that a belt of lion skin should be worn, or, failing those that the plague should be frightened away with strong smells. Some people carried bunches of sweet smelling flowers, or kept a goat in the bedroom hoping that its powerful smell would drive away the disease.

This nursery rhyme may be about the Black Death:

Ring-a-ring o' Roses	red boils on the skin
A pocketful of posies	flowers to keep away the plague
Tishoo, Tishoo,	sneezing was a sign of the plague
We all fall down.	DEAD!

Things to do

1 *Complete these sentences using the words in the box.*

Another name for the Black Death is ....

Large .... spots covered the bodies of the plague victims.

The village of .... was never lived in again.

The germs which caused the Black Death were spread by ....

rat fleas, Tusmore, Bubonic Plague, black

2 *How would a medieval doctor deal with an infectious disease like the plague?*
How would your doctor today deal with an infectious disease?

3 *How do the words of the nursery rhyme "Ring-a-ring o' Roses" describe the Black Death?*

3 Drink and be merry

4 Prayer and punishment to keep away the plague

13 Gardens

1 A garden

called "knots", as you can see in the drawing. They did not mix the flowers in each pattern, but kept the same types and the same colours together. So, from an upstairs window the flower garden looked like a brightly patterned carpet. Rich merchants carried small bunches of sweet smelling pinks and carnations when they walked in the town to hide the nasty smells of the town streets. Their wives used cut flowers to make perfume and flowers also provided food for the swarms of bees kept by townsmen in their gardens. They used the honey which the bees made to sweeten food, for very little sugar was available in those days. The townsmen did not have much choice of vegetables and fruit to grow in their gardens, for many of the plants we know today did not come to Great Britain until

2 A flower knot

Town gardens were small because land was expensive within the walls. To make the best use of their small gardens, towns-people only grew vegetables, fruit, herbs and flowers. They did not have room for open spaces, lawns or even large trees, for they used all the garden to grow food or their favourite flowers. Townspeople protected their gardens from the wind and from robbers by a high stone wall as you can see in the picture. Narrow gravel paths or low hedges about ten inches high, ran between the beds of soil. A few people decorated their gardens with small yew trees, cut to the shape of birds or animals, but everyone tried to grow beautiful flowers. Their favourites were stocks, carnations, clove-scented pinks, and wall-flowers. They planted them in patterns after the Middle Ages. The housewife often had to make do with cabbages, leeks and apples from her own garden, but in order to cook tasty meals, added many of the herbs she grew as well. In the spring she planted garlic, rosemary, sage, thyme, mint and parsley. Then in summer she picked, dried and stored the herbs in jars like those in the picture opposite. She used these herbs for making sauces to drown the salty taste of the meat in winter. Farmers could not store enough food for their cattle during the winter and so they killed the animals at the beginning of the autumn. Housewives stopped the meat from going rotten by keeping it in salt, but as this made it taste nasty the strong flavour of herbs helped to give the meat a better flavour. Most housewives used herbs as simple cures for everyday illnesses. From a collection of letters which Margaret Paston wrote to her husband we know that she had far more faith in her own recipes than in all the medicines given by London doctors. She used crowsfoot root to cure toothache, and blue periwinkle flowers for cramp in the legs. Margaret had collected many of her cures from friends and relations, like the cure for convulsions and fits, "best sherry, mixed with herbs and flowers and distilled". A doctor visiting patients suffering from the Plague often wore a strange hat filled with herbs and shaped like a bird's beak. This was supposed to stop the doctor from catching the Plague disease and you can see his picture opposite.

3   Doctor wearing plague costume

5   A herb store room

4   Bees

Things to do

1   *Complete these sentences using the words in the box.*
Town gardens were .... because land was expensive within the walls.
Townsfolk used all the space in their gardens to grow .... or their favourite ....
They used .... to sweeten food, and .... to hide the salty taste of meat in winter.

honey, food, small, flowers, herbs

2   *Draw or trace the flower knot pattern and then colour it.*

31

14 Festivals

1 Well dressing

2 Plague cottage at Eyam

Twenty-five days on the medieval calendar were coloured red and called Red Letter Days. They were holidays for the townspeople. They included May Day, Midsummer Day, Hallowe'en, and Shrove Tuesday as well as our own holidays of Easter and Christmas Day. But this was not all, for each town had its own celebrations as well. On those days they gave thanks for the wise people who had lived there before them, or for good luck which had helped the town. Three of these local festivals still take place, as you can see from the pictures. In 1349 Tissington, in Derbyshire, escaped the Black Death which killed over half the people in the rest of the county. There were no deaths because of the pure water in Tissington's five wells. So each year on Ascension Day, the people of Tissington decorate these wells and give thanks for the safety of their town from the Plague. The ceremony of decorating the wells is called "well dressing". Townsfolk put a wooden frame behind the well and cover the wood in soft clay. Then they stick flowers, feathers and berries onto the clay to make a picture, which is usually a Bible scene. You can see a picture of one of the wells decorated in a recent festival. Another festival in Derbyshire, this time at Eyam, remembers great bravery and unselfishness there at the time of the Plague. When the local tailor caught the Plague from a parcel of clothing sent from London, the people said that they would have no contact with their neighbouring villages for twelve months. In this way they stopped the Plague spreading to the countryside around. The Vicar of Eyam, William Mompesson, held his church services in the open air at Cucklett Delf. He thought, quite rightly, that if people met inside the church, the Plague would spread more easily. Each year people in Eyam go to a service held in the Delf on Plague Sunday, the first Sunday in August. They give thanks for the courage of all the townsmen, and remember the two hundred and fifty who died in the year of the Plague. In Abbots Bromley the reason for the Horn Dance Festival held each September happened many years before the Plague. In the Stone Age, men worshipped a popular horned god of Hunting and Death. Later, the Christians called him Saint Nicholas, and later still he became Father Christmas, with the horns now on his reindeer. The dancers dance slowly, carrying deer antlers on short poles, round all the farms near Abbots Bromley. At each stopping point they pray for good crops for the next year.

3   Abbots Bromley Horn Dance Festival

Things to do

1   *Complete these sentences using the words in the box.*

The medieval calendar had .... days coloured red, called .... Days.

Pure water in the five wells at .... saved the town from the ....

Plague came to .... in a parcel of clothing sent from ....

Red Letter, Tissington, twenty-five, Plague, Eyam, London

15 Witches

1 Mother Shipton

2 Witches making a storm

Most medieval townsmen believed in witches. At first people thought the witches' power came from kind and good spirits. The witches, or wise women, treated the illnesses and listened to the problems of poor people who could not afford to pay the doctors' expensive fees.

Witches made medicines from herbs and some of the medicine they handed out was useful. For example, a Shropshire witch gave foxglove tea to her patients with heart trouble. The foxglove, sometimes called "the witches' glove", contains a drug still used to cure heart disease today. Witches found or "conjured" lost objects by magic. So in a churchwarden's accounts at Burfield we read that he, "paid for the ingoing to Burfield to the Conjurer [witch] for to make enquiry for the Communion Cloth lost out of the church". Some witches could see into the future. Mother Shipton, a witch who lived in Yorkshire, was famous for her prophecies. She described road accidents: "Carriages without horses shall go/And accidents fill the world with woe"; and radio, "Around the world thoughts shall fly/Within the twinkling of an eye". Though she got some things wrong (she said that the world would end in 1891), she seems to have been a wise and thoughtful person.

Towards the end of the Middle Ages, townsmen puzzled at all the disasters around them, such as bad harvests, ships lost at sea and the Black Death. Why had these terrible things happened? In this worrying time people looked for someone to blame. They said that witches, who seemed to know all about magic, caused the trouble. So now, instead of thinking that a witch was a kind and helpful woman, they said she was evil and her power came from the Devil himself. They listened to stories of witches causing storms at sea, spoiling crops with hailstorms, bewitching cattle, even spreading the Black Death through the towns. On Holy Island they "buried 16 July, William Cleugh, bewitched to death". When a witch was supposed to be helping the devil, people said he gave her a demon, in the form of a cat, to carry out her wicked orders. So, many lonely old women with cats were blamed for accidents and bad luck in towns and villages. It was easy for townsfolk to make up a story about a neighbour they did not like and have her killed because they said she was a witch. In Lancashire, four old women were killed after a boy said he saw them turn into greyhounds. It was only after they were dead that he confessed that he was lying. The "test" for a witch was to see if she floated on water, and the punishment for a witch was always death. As late as 1926 a Dorset man accused his neighbour of bewitching his pig! So you can see that belief in witches' magic powers lasted long after the end of the Middle Ages.

Things to do

1 *Complete these sentences using the words in the box.*

Most medieval townsmen believed in ....

Witches made .... for poor people who could not afford to pay the doctors' fees.

A .... found lost objects by magic.

.... could see into the future.

People blamed witches for .... and bad luck in their towns.

The punishment for a witch was always ....

medicines, Mother Shipton, witches, death, conjurer, accidents

2 *How did a wise woman, or witch, help the townsfolk?*
3 *Why did people punish witches towards the end of the Middle Ages?*

3 Witches with their cats

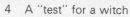
4 A "test" for a witch

16 The Canterbury Pilgrims

1   Travelling to Canterbury

In medieval times most people travelled at least once to an important religious place. The journey, called a pilgrimage, showed that they were good Christians, willing to spend time and money on their religion. Usually the pilgrims travelled together for company and for safety against robbers. The journey was rather like a holiday, because the pilgrims saw new towns and had a change from their daily work. Priests did not like such light-heartedness, and one in Canterbury complained, "what with the noise of their singing, and with the sound of their piping and with the jangling of their Canterbury bells and with the barking out of dogs after them, they make more noise than if the King came!"

Pilgrims went to see colourful decorated buildings called shrines. The shrines held "relics" or objects which had once belonged to a saint, for example his comb or shoe, or tooth, or even a bone from his body. People believed that miracles cured the illnesses of pilgrims who touched these relics. The monks looking after the relics and the shrines made a lot of money from the pilgrims and some monks even "invented" relics to increase their takings. There were so many "genuine thorns" from Jesus's Crown of Thorns that even medieval writers said that it must have been a hedge and not a crown!

The most famous shrine in England was Archbishop Thomas à Becket's tomb at Canterbury. (Henry II's knights murdered the Archbishop in Canterbury Cathedral.) Geoffrey Chaucer, a great poet of this time, wrote a long poem about a group of Canterbury pilgrims and the stories they told each other on the journey. Chaucer had made the pilgrimage himself and in his poem describes some of the pilgrims he met. Three of them, a prioress, a friar and a doctor are shown at the foot of the next page. The monks and people of Canterbury were well organised to look after the religious tourists. There was a set tour of the Holy Places which dealt quickly with the long queues in order to allow as many pilgrims as possible to see the shrine. Stalls sold souvenir badges of St Thomas's Shrine for pilgrims to show their friends at home. Some pilgrims hired horses for their journey to Canterbury from London and Rochester. To guard against thieves and vandals amongst the visitors, each hired horse was branded with the owner's mark in case it was stolen. Monks warned the pilgrims not to chip pieces of stone from the shrine or, as some noblemen had tried, carve their coats of arms on the buildings. The shrine itself was the most exciting part of the pilgrimage. In flickering candlelight, to the sound of bells, a monk lifted the cover and pointed to the treasures inside it. A pilgrim from Venice in Italy described the shrine in the following words, "its great size is wholly covered with plates of pure gold, yet the gold is scarcely seen because it is covered with precious stones, sapphires, diamonds, rubies and emeralds". It was certainly worth making the journey to Canterbury to see this shrine.

Things to do

1 Complete these sentences using the words in the box.

A journey to an important religious place was called a ....

Shrines held .... which had once belonged to a saint.

Some monks invented relics to make more ....

The most famous shrine in England was Archbishop .... tomb at ....

> Becket's, relics, money, pilgrimage, Canterbury

2 Ask your teacher to tell you the story of the murder of Archbishop Becket.

2 Doctor

Friar

Prioress

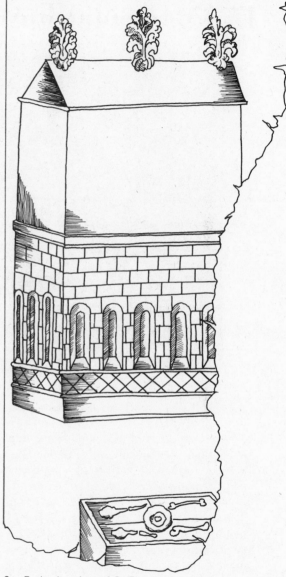

3 Early drawing of St Thomas' shrine

17 Roads and Travellers

1   The traveller has a meal at the House of Rest Inn

Although maps of medieval England show a great number of roads they were little better than present day farm tracks. They had no surface of stones but were just made of hardpacked clay or soil. It is easy to see why a traveller described them as "feet deep in mud in winter and choked by dust in summer". Not only the weather destroyed the roads. Farmers sometimes decided to plough across them, and at Aylesbury the local miller dug a large hole in the highway. Unfortunately, it filled with water and a glove seller fell into it and drowned. In court, the jury set the miller free for they said there was nowhere else for a miller to get the clay he needed! The roads should have been wide enough for sixteen armed knights to ride side by side, but most were much narrower than this. Bushes and trees grew in the clear space which the law said should be two hundred feet wide on each side of the road. The idea of this was to stop robbers hiding near the roadside and ambushing travellers on the road. To protect themselves from thieves, and have companions able to help them if they got into difficulties, medieval townsmen travelled in groups and put their faith in St Christopher, the travellers' saint. St Christopher is usually shown helping people across a river. Rivers were the main obstacles for travellers. There were not many bridges because they were expensive to build. Rich men gave money to build them, usually in their wills, and in the Chapel on the bridge at Wakefield travellers gave thanks for the soul of this bridge builder. The traveller paid a local guide to choose the safest and easiest route. The guide alone could lead the way for there were no signposts and roads and bridges were often washed away overnight in thunderstorms. Sir Thomas Howard paid two pence for a guide to take him across the Wash, a short cut into Lincolnshire from Norwich. This was a dangerous crossing as King John had found to his cost! Travel was slow by modern standards, for most people walked. Rich men on horses could cover thirty miles a day, and messengers changing horses frequently, could travel twice that distance in the same time. All, except these messengers, avoided the roads at night. People called those out at dark "nightwalkers against the peace"! There were many overnight stops on long journeys (five or six between York and London) and travellers stayed at inns for food and shelter. It also took a long time to move goods between towns, for townsmen carried

38

everything on packhorses or wagons. The wagons had large wheels, their rims studded with big nails to grip the road surfaces when they were slippy. The wagons and the packhorses moved slowly with their drivers walking beside them. No honest medieval man rode in a cart, for carts carried criminals to their execution! So, many people used the roads of medieval England. Large households like those of Bishop Swinfield and Lady Anne Mowbray travelled along with merchants, tramps, beggars, pilgrims, judges and long strings of packhorses and wagons.

Things to do

1   *Complete these sentences using the words in the box.*
    Medieval roads were little better than present day ....
    .... ambushed travellers on the road.
    St .... was the travellers' saint.
    .... were the main obstacles for travellers.

> rivers, Christopher, farm tracks, robbers

2   *Ask your teacher to tell you how King John lost his crown in The Wash.*
3   *Make a list of the dangers and problems faced by the traveller in medieval days.*

3   Wine barrels on a wagon

4   A prisoner travels in a cart

2   St Christopher

18 London Bridge

1 Old London Bridge

2 Houses on Old London Bridge

It was difficult to build bridges over wide or swift flowing rivers in medieval times. Travellers on foot used the ferries, but it was hard to load and unload heavy wagons and packhorses from small ferry boats. They had to make extra long journeys to cross by the few bridges that had been built. If a town had a bridge it was very proud of the fact and gained a lot of trade from travellers using the bridge. Until medieval times London had a bridge built of wood. The water rotted its supports, occasionally it caught fire, and once in 1014, raiders from Scandinavia put ropes round the piers and rowed downstream dragging the whole bridge into the water. It fell down just as it says in the Nursery Rhyme! Londoners wanted a strong bridge that would last a long time. They wanted a bridge made of stone. In 1176 Peter de Colechurch, a local priest, started to build the first stone bridge across the River Thames at London. His bridge took thirty-three years to finish and became one of the marvels of medieval Europe. The Bridge had twenty narrow arches held up by stone piers built in mid-river. These piers needed protection from the fast moving waters of the River Thames. The builder put long wooden islands, called starlings, around each stone pier. The river had to force its way through the narrow gaps between these islands. At some states of the tide the islands held the water back until it was five feet higher on one side, and there were waterfalls under the arches. Londoners enjoyed a game of shooting down these waterfalls in small boats, but it was dangerous and people drowned this way. There was a wooden drawbridge to let tall ships pass through. The drawbridge could also be lifted up to stop rebels and attackers from crossing the river to reach the City. A number of poles on Drawbridge Gate often carried the heads of traitors. Visitors to London paid the Bridge Toll of a quarter penny for walkers or one penny for horsemen just to see these heads! Wooden houses built on the Bridge made the roadway very narrow. The houses, crammed into a small space, overhung the river and sometimes fell down into it. As well as houses, there were inns, one hundred and thirty shops and a Chapel named after St Thomas à Becket, the Archbishop of Canterbury murdered a few years before Peter de Colechurch started his Bridge. Peter was buried in the Chapel. The rents from the Bridge houses and shops, and tolls charged on people and goods passing under or over the Bridge paid for Peter's work. Londoners were proud of their famous Bridge and often left some money in their wills "to God and The Bridge". As the years went on the amount of money "owned" by London Bridge grew into a large sum. When, over 600 years later a new bridge replaced Peter's Bridge, this money was used to build it. The latest London Bridge, opened in 1973, is shown in the picture. Only three arches are needed instead of Peter's twenty and tall ships no longer pass upstream.

3   London Bridge in 1973

4   Traitors' heads on Drawbridge Gate

Things to do

1   *Complete these sentences using the words in the box.*

.... built a stone bridge across the Thames.

.... heads were stuck on poles on Drawbridge Gate.

Wooden .... on the Bridge made the roadway very narrow.

> traitors', houses, Peter de Colechurch

2   *Look at the pictures of London Bridge and point out some differences between the Old Bridge and the new Bridge.*

3   *Draw or trace Old London Bridge.*

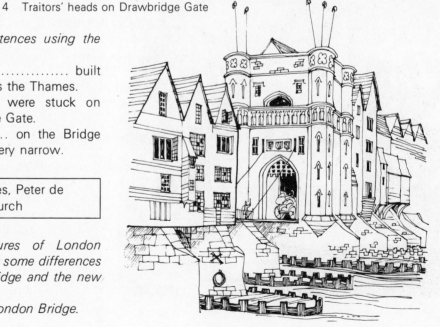

19 Wat Tyler

1 King Richard II listens to petitions

2 "When Adam delved and Eve span . . ."

After the Black Death there were fewer peasants to work on the land. The peasants grumbled because the landowners forced them to work harder and would not let them become freemen. Townsmen too grumbled about their low wages and blamed all their problems on the government. They sent many petitions to young King Richard II but, although he promised to help, he never kept his promises. Finally, the government ordered everyone in the country over the age of fifteen to pay a poll tax of five pence a year. The poll tax came as the last straw to the working people and many decided that they would not pay.

A priest called John Ball told them that this was the right decision, for he told people to ask whether poor peasants should pay poll taxes to keep the nobles and churchmen rich. Wat Tyler, a Kentish farmer, thought the same as John Ball, and he became the leader of the unhappy peasants when the people of his village killed the tax collector. News of the revolt spread quickly and the peasants of Kent and Essex agreed to march to London and tell the King their troubles. Twenty thousand men camped on Blackheath, near London, and listened to John Ball preaching against the rich men. "By what right do rich lords wear fine clothes and live in big houses while their peasants work in the fields in all weathers?"

"When Adam delved, and Eve span,
Who was then a gentleman?"

When they reached London itself, they went wild and burnt important buildings, murdered the Archbishop of Canterbury in the Tower of London, and demanded to meet King Richard. Officials arranged a meeting with Richard at Smithfield, outside the City Walls. Wat Tyler was by now full of his own importance as leader of the peasant mob and his manner towards Richard was rude and bullying. When he made a movement as if to draw his dagger, William Walworth, the Mayor of London, and another knight rushed towards him and killed him. (It is said that the sword on the City of London's Coat of Arms is a copy of the one that killed Tyler.) This was a very dangerous moment for the King as the Kentish archers were ready to kill him and the Mayor in revenge for Tyler's murder. With great bravery Richard rode towards the angry mob shouting, "I am your leader, I am your King. It is me

3   Death of Wat Tyler

4   Coat of Arms of the City of London

you should follow." Slowly the crowd left Smithfield and the danger to the King passed. His soldiers were waiting for the rebels as they left London, but many escaped back to their villages in Essex and Kent. Richard sent his soldiers there to burn the peasants' houses and kill their leaders, including John Ball. Richard was now saying to the peasants, "Villeins [peasants] you were, and villeins you are; in bondage you shall abide." Soon after this, the nobles themselves rebelled against Richard and made his cousin Henry king instead. Richard was kept in the Tower of London and died there within a year. The official story said that he refused to eat and starved to death, but some say he was poisoned.

Things to do

1   Complete these sentences using the words in the box.

.... preached to the peasants on Blackheath.
The peasant mob met Richard at ....
Wat Tyler was killed by the .... and a knight.
Richard punished the peasants and killed their ....

> Mayor of London, leaders,
> John Ball, Smithfield

2   Describe the scene when Wat Tyler met Richard II at Smithfield.

3   What was a poll tax? Everyone had to pay the same amount. Was this fair?

20 Church Brasses

1 Sir Roger de Trumpington

In the Middle Ages most dead people were buried in the Churchyard. However, rich families buried their relatives in stone chests and kept them inside the Church. They carved a life sized stone or alabaster statue of the dead person lying on top of the chest. As time went on there wasn't any more room for tomb chests inside the Church so they put the bodies beneath the floor and cut a figure into the flat stone lid. The stone was easily damaged and so people looked for a harder material for the picture, and chose brass. These brass pictures were put on the floor over the coffin or, sometimes, on the walls of the Church so that the families would be remembered for ever. The brasses show the buried person dressed in the clothes he usually wore. Amongst those still un-damaged today are knights in armour, wives, craftsmen and children. The brass of Sir Roger at Trumpington near Cambridge shows him wearing a Crusader's suit of chain mail. A cloth coat covers his armour to keep him cool in the sun and he carries a heavy sword, a shield with a trumpet drawn on it and his feet rest on a dog.

At Hever in Kent, Margaret Cheyne's brass shows the cloak she wore over her long dress. A short veil covers her hair which is tied up in nets on each side of her head. Craftsmen and traders also paid to have brasses made. We can still see what a fishmonger at Taplow, a glove

2 Margaret Cheyne

maker at Fletching and even a criminal at Lindfield looked like from their brasses. We know what they made or sold as their feet rest upon something connected with their job. Wine merchants have a barrel of wine and at Northleach, a tailor of Gloucester rests by a pair of scissors. Children are often shown on the brasses of a whole family. The older ones who had

3   The children of Robert Manfield

4   Chrysom baby

5   The tailor of Gloucester

died before the group was drawn wear a sheet knotted at head and feet called a shroud. In the brass at Taplow of the children of Robert Manfield, Richard and Isabel on the left, alive at the time the brass was made, wear ordinary clothes. Their dead brother John on the right wears a shroud and has a cross on his head. The saddest brasses are those of babies who died very young. All babies were wrapped in a special cloth, called a chrysom for the first month of their life. If they died during that time they were buried in this chrysom. You can see in the picture the brass of a chrysom baby at Merstham in Surrey with a small bib pinned under its chin.

Things to do

You can make some interesting black and white pictures by putting a sheet of thin paper over a church brass, and crayoning gently with a stick of hard black wax crayon. Remember to ask for permission from the priest before you make a brass rubbing in a Church.

21 Further Study

York
Wakefield
Liverpool
Conway
Chester
Eyam
Tissington
Abbots
Bromley
King's Lynn
Norwich
Worcester
Hereford
Cambridge
Framlingham
Ross on Wye
Gloucester
Trumpington
Thaxted
Northleach
Aylesbury
Oxford
Taplow
LONDON
Bristol
Merstham
Hever
Lindfield
Rochester
Canterbury
Fletching

1 Towns mentioned in this book

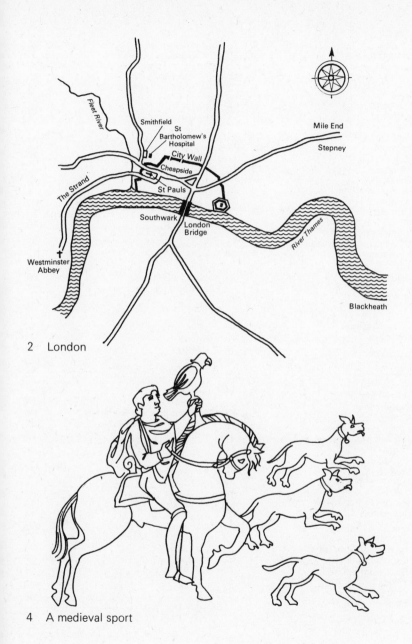

2 London

3 London Bridge

5 Margaret Peyton

4 A medieval sport

2 *London*
Which of the names on this map of London can you connect with Wat Tyler or with Lady Anne Mowbray?

3 *London Bridge*
Which river did this Bridge cross and what can you say about the buildings on the Bridge?

4 *A medieval sport*
This was a very popular sport in medieval times. Can you say why the bird has a hood over its head and what the dogs were used for?

5 *Margaret Peyton*
Where in a medieval town would you look for brass pictures like this one of Margaret Peyton? What is the name of the head-dress she wears and can you tell from her clothes if she was rich or poor?

Index